EARTH-FRIENDLY
ENERGY

RON FRIDELL

LERNER PUBLICATIONS COMPANY · MINNEAPOLIS

Lerner Publications Company
A division of Lerner Publishing Group, Inc.
241 First Avenue North
Minneapolis, MN 55401 U.S.A.

Website address: www.lernerbooks.com

Library of Congress Cataloging-in-Publication Data

Fridell, Ron.
    Earth-friendly energy / by Ron Fridell.
        p.   cm. — (Saving our living earth)
    Includes bibliographical references and index.
    ISBN 978-0-8225-7563-4 (lib. bdg. : alk. paper)
    1. renewable energy sources—Juvenile literature. 2. Fossil fuels—Environmental aspects—Juvenile literature. 3. Green movement. I. Title.
TJ808.2.F75 2009
333.79—dc22   2007035924

Manufactured in the United States of America
1 2 3 4 5 6 — DP — 14 13 12 11 10 09

CONTENTS

INTRODUCTION 4

BEYOND FOSSIL FUELS 6

SOLAR POWER 12

WIND POWER 26

WATER POWER 36

EARTH POWER 44

BIOFUELS 50

INTO THE FUTURE 54

Going Green 64
Glossary 66
Source Notes 67
Selected Bibliography 68
Further Reading 69
Index 70

INTRODUCTION

Imagine that you're standing on a street corner in a big city. Cars and buses rumble by. Signs twinkle and flash. Smells from nearby restaurants make your mouth water. The air is alive with energy.

Have you ever asked yourself, *"Where does all this energy come from?"* Not the food energy that powers your body—but the manufactured energy that powers the world.

Oil helps cars and buses run. Coal helps create electricity that sets signs flashing. And natural gas heats restaurant ovens and grills. Oil, coal, and

Top: Vehicles powered by fossil fuels rumble down Fifth Avenue in New York City. *Right:* A coal-burning power plant in Spain spews smoke into the air. *Opposite page:* Solar panels on the roof of a home collect energy from the sun.

natural gas are fossil fuels. They formed underground from plants and animals that died millions of years ago. Right now most manufactured energy comes from fossil fuels. But they won't last forever. Experts say we will run out of oil and natural gas before the century ends.

Limited supplies are one good reason why we need to replace fossil fuels with other forms of energy. Environmental concerns are another. Fossil fuels cause pollution when we use them. And before we can use them, we have to dig into the ground to get at them. Digging into the ground can harm the land. We need to replace fossil fuels with other kinds of energy that will not run out and will not harm the planet.

Experts say we will run out of oil and natural gas before the century ends.

Many scientists, engineers, inventors, businesspeople, volunteers, and political leaders are focusing on this challenge. They are concentrating on Earth-friendly energy sources: solar power, wind power, water power, and Earth power. You can play a part in this challenge. Keep that in mind as we look at how Earth-friendly energy sources are replacing fossil fuels around the world.

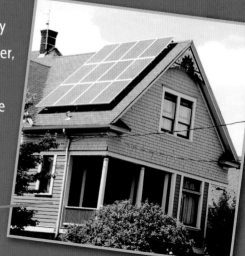

CHAPTER ONE

BEYOND FOSSIL FUELS

Shangma Huangtou is a village in the north China province of Shanxi. One night in 2006, the ground in Shangma Huangtou began to shake. *Earthquake!* the villagers thought as the ground beneath their feet opened wide.

But it was not an earthquake that split the earth that night in China. It was a coal sink. For years coal miners had been digging deep into the earth nearby, trying to get at the coal that lay underground. Sometimes they used dynamite to break apart deposits of coal. Finally, the earth cracked open as a result of the mining.

Other villages in China have suffered because of coal mining too. Some keep splitting and sinking. Others are covered by a fog of poisoned air from coal fires raging deep underground. These villages have become wastelands. The residents have had to leave.

Villages in China have suffered because of coal mining.

PRODUCERS POLLUTE

The producers of fossil fuel energy are partly to blame for the damage fossil fuels are causing to the environment. Among them are the people who own and operate power plants that make electricity. Some power plants produce electricity by burning natural gas or oil. But most burn coal. Plants that burn coal are known as coal-fired power plants.

A coal-fired power plant in Virginia provides electricity for area homes and businesses. Coal-fired power plants produce much-needed energy—but they are also responsible for a great deal of pollution.

Workers make repairs to the blades on this steam turbine. When the blades spin, they provide energy to generate electricity.

Coal-fired power plants burn coal that has been crushed to a fine dust. The burning coal dust superheats water and turns it into steam. The steam shoots through pipes to turn steam turbines. Steam turbines are heat engines that work something like propellers or fans. They have rotating blades. As steam turns the steam turbines' blades, the turbines' shafts spin. The spinning shafts drive generators—machines that produce electricity.

The electricity then flows through a grid, or network, of power lines to substations in cities and towns. From each substation, the electricity is delivered to individual homes and businesses.

Coal-fired power plants are a

DID YOU KNOW?

Steam turbines are not just used in power plants. They have been used to power locomotives, ships on oceans and rivers, and even automobiles.

major source of air pollution. As they burn coal, they release exhaust gases through their smokestacks. Exhaust gases are very dirty. They contain pollutants such as sulfur dioxide, nitrous oxide, and mercury. These pollutants spread widely. They travel hundreds of miles on the wind. When inhaled, they can cause health problems that range from wheezing and chest pains to asthma attacks and inflamed lungs.

CONSUMERS POLLUTE

Consumers—the people who use fossil fuels—must share the blame for the world's air pollution problems. Furnaces and water heaters burn natural gas, while car motors burn gasoline made from oil. As a result, fossil fuel fumes are continually released from millions of homes and cars.

Homes, cars, and power plants dump billions of tons of the pollutant carbon dioxide (CO_2) into the air each year. They also produce other pollutants such as methane and nitrous oxide. The result? Tens of thousands of people each year get sick from these pollutants. Some even die.

PLANET EARTH HEATS UP

These pollutants threaten the health of the planet as well.

WHAT'S IN A BARREL OF OIL?

Every day around the world we use about 200 million barrels of oil. A barrel of oil gives us about 20 gallons (75 liters) of gasoline. That's a little more than what's needed to fill an average car's gas tank. So every time we fill our cars with gas, we use about a barrel of oil.

WORLD CO$_2$ POLLUTION

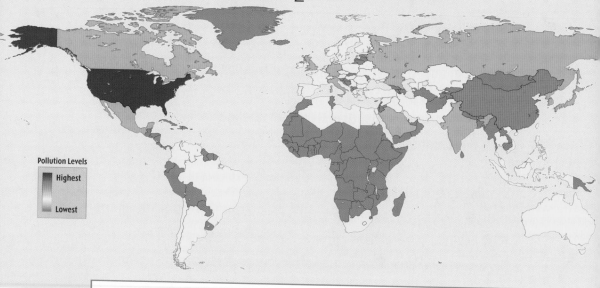

Pollution Levels
Highest
Lowest

This map shows the amounts of CO$_2$ pollution released by countries around the world. How much CO$_2$ does your country produce?

WHO USES THE MOST ENERGY?

The richer and more advanced a nation is, the bigger the share of the world's energy it uses. The United States uses more energy than any other country. It has only 6 percent of the world's population, yet it uses 25 percent of the world's total fossil fuel energy supply.

CO$_2$ builds up in Earth's atmosphere. When it builds up, it traps heat near Earth. The sun shines on Earth. Some of the sun's heat soaks into the ground. And some of it escapes into outer space. But CO$_2$ prevents heat from escaping. It holds heat near Earth. This makes Earth's temperature gradually rise. The gradual rising of Earth's temperature is known as global warming.

Global warming is severely harming Earth. The rising temperature is changing the planet's climate, or usual weather patterns. The ice caps at the North Pole and South Pole have started to melt. The melting is releasing more water into the oceans. This means that sea levels will rise and coastlines could be flooded. The warmer temperatures also may cause severe weather. That's because warm air feeds hurricanes, tornadoes, and other storms.

GREENHOUSE GASES

CO_2 and other air pollutants are called greenhouse gases. That's because they act like the glass in a greenhouse, holding in heat from the sun.

No one can say for sure what long-term effects global warming will have. But one thing is certain: humans are changing the planet's climate. Scientists warn everyone, producers and consumers alike, to stop dumping so much CO_2 and other pollutants into the atmosphere.

WHAT CAN WE DO?

We must move beyond fossil fuels as quickly as possible. We must replace them with new energy sources that don't pollute the air and won't run out.

Because fossil fuels take millions of years to form, they can't be replaced. Once they're depleted, they're gone for good. That makes coal, oil, and natural gas nonrenewable energy sources.

Renewable energy sources, on the other hand, won't get depleted and disappear. What's more, they are Earth friendly. They don't cause as much damage to the land. And using them won't contribute to global warming. Where do these renewable, Earth-friendly energies come from? Read on to find out.

CHAPTER TWO

SOLAR POWER

Step outside on a warm, breezy day. Right away you'll feel two Earth-friendly energy sources all around you: the blowing wind and the heat from the sun. Other Earth-friendly, renewable energy sources include moving water, heat from Earth's core, and plants such as prairie grasses.

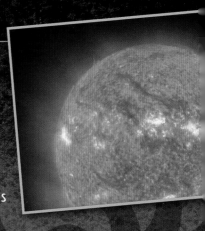

The most powerful Earth-friendly energy source of all is the sun.

SPEEDING PHOTONS

The most powerful Earth-friendly energy source of all is the sun. The sun's core creates heat so intense that it splits atoms. When atoms break apart at the sun's core, they fire off particles called photons.

The solar energy that reaches Earth is made of waves of photons carrying heat and light energy. These waves radiate through outer space until they enter Earth's atmosphere and strike the surface.

WHAT IS AN ATOM?

An atom is the smallest part of a substance. Atoms are the building blocks of matter. Atoms and particles called molecules make up everything that exists on Earth.

The sun provides the energy that drives many of Earth's natural forces, such as wind and climate. People are learning how to capture the sun's power to use as an Earth-friendly energy source. *Left:* Immense explosions on the sun, called solar flares, can be detected on Earth, which lies 91 million miles (146 million km) away.

Oceans, lakes, rivers, land, and air absorb these waves and become warmer. Then winds and ocean currents spread this solar heat around the world. In the space of a single minute, enough photons strike the planet to supply all our energy needs for an entire year, if we could only harness all that solar energy.

14

A PHOTON'S LONG JOURNEY

It takes a photon a long time—about one hundred thousand years—to get from the core of the sun to its surface. By comparison, the photon's trip through space to Earth is a whiz. It travels the 91 million miles (146 million kilometers) from the sun to Earth's surface in only about eight minutes. In space, photons travel at the speed of light: 186,287 miles (299,800 km) per second.

The sun warms these tranquil waters in Oahu, Hawaii.

Solar panels on the roof of a house in Oxford, England, collect the sun's heat to make energy for the home.

SOLAR PANELS

We have a long way to go before we could ever supply all our energy needs from the sun. Our technology isn't efficient enough yet. But we are making progress.

You may have seen flat black or blue panels mounted on roofs and in backyards. These panels are banks of solar cells. They collect energy from sunlight and convert it into electricity to power homes.

Businesses also use solar cells. The shipping business FedEx has its own building at the Oakland, California, airport. One day someone had a bright idea, in more ways than one. For years the sun had been shining brightly on the building's roof. Why not take advantage of all that free solar power? The company mounted 81,000 square feet (7,500 square meters) of solar panels on that roof. They supply 80 percent of the building's energy needs.

SOLAR POWER PLANTS

What happens when you hook thousands of solar panels together and collect their combined power? You have a solar power plant. Solar power plants are an Earth-friendly alternative to conventional power plants. They don't burn coal, oil, or natural gas, so they don't pollute the air.

Some states generate part of their electricity in solar power plants. The state of Arizona generates about I percent of its electricity in this way.

A new Arizona project features an advanced solar technology called concentrators. Concentrators are a little like magnifying glasses. They gather in and focus a wide area of sunlight onto a small area of solar cells.

A solar power plant in the sunny Mojave Desert generates plenty of clean and renewable energy.

ANCIENT SUN AND FIRE

The idea of concentrating the sun's energy is not a new one. It has been around since ancient times. Historians believe that the Greek mathematician and physician Archimedes (287–212 B.C.) used mirrors to concentrate the sun's power. This concentrated power was used to set attacking Roman ships on fire.

These concentrators automatically follow the sun as it moves across the sky. That way they take maximum advantage of the entire day's sunlight, from dawn to dusk.

SOLAR-POWERED HOMES

How would you like your own personal solar power plant? Some states encourage homeowners to go solar by giving them breaks on their income taxes. As a result, more homeowners are installing rooftop solar panels every day.

California is a leader in solar-generated electricity. Many California celebrities have gone solar. They include actors Leonardo DiCaprio and Alicia Silverstone, musician Carlos Santana, and former baseball pitcher Tom Seaver. Actor Edward Norton speaks out for solar power in Los Angeles. He urges his fellow celebrities to install solar panels on their homes.

SOLAR TRANSPORT

Electricity isn't the only form of energy solar panels can produce. Solar panels also power spacecraft, cars, planes, and boats. In December 2006, a 46-foot-long (14 m) solar-powered boat called *sun21* sailed from Spain. Its crew was on a mission to make the world's first transatlantic solar-powered journey. They succeeded when they landed on the Caribbean island of Martinique on February 2, 2007.

Throughout the boat's journey, its motor did not use a single drop of fossil fuel. It ran entirely on electricity generated by solar panels. Batteries on

17

The *sun21* nears Manhattan, New York, after completing its transatlantic journey.

board stored away extra energy on sunny days to use at night and on cloudy days. The stored energy in the *sun21*'s batteries kept the boat moving day and night.

The weather cooperated, but the journey was not always smooth. Crew members kept a diary. Here is part of one entry:

> In the late afternoon, our captain . . . notices a monstrous Chinese tanker [that] approaches us at a considerable speed. . . . [W]e have to change our course southwards in order to escape a collision. . . . Now, just before sunset, we watch dolphins again throwing themselves high up in the evening sky.

SOLAR POWER FOR SOLDIERS

How about using solar power to help soldiers fight wars? The U.S. Army is calling for companies to build renewable-energy power stations that will generate electricity for soldiers fighting in remote areas of Iraq. The stations will use a combination of solar and wind power to provide electricity.

Soldiers in remote areas typically rely on generators that burn diesel fuel to generate electrical power. But diesel generators are noisy. They call attention to soldiers' positions. In a war, that means telling the enemy where you are. Using solar panels even part of the time cuts down on the noise that puts soldiers' lives in danger.

Soldiers already use foldout solar panels to recharge batteries in remote areas. Foldout solar panels are lightweight, flexible, and weatherproof. They can recharge everything electric, from flashlights to night-vision goggles to laptop computers. That means soldiers don't have to haul around so many heavy, disposable batteries anymore. The more soldiers can rely on solar power, the safer they will be.

Foldout solar panels can be a lifesaver for soldiers serving in military operations around the world.

SOLAR HEAT

Solar technology also heats water and air in buildings. Solar collectors are the key. Collectors gather the sun's heat and transfer it to where it's needed.

The heat can be transferred to a water storage tank, such as a water heater. Homes with solar water heaters still use electricity or natural gas to heat water. But they use much less of it. Solar heat provides about two-thirds of the energy needed to supply hot water.

Some solar-heating systems use solar collectors to heat air. Fans or heat pumps run the heated air into the building. Other systems don't use solar collectors at all. Instead, the houses are designed to take advantage of the sunlight shining on them. Large windows on the south side of a house, where the sun shines most, bring in lots of heat. The floors and walls can be made of materials that absorb warmth during the day and release heat at night, when it's needed most.

20

PEOPLE WITHOUT POWER

Have you ever been in a blackout, where the electricity suddenly goes out and the night turns black? Then you know how about 2 billion of the planet's 6.6 billion

Homes can be specially designed to take full advantage of the sun's energy. Sun provides heat and light for plants in this Earth-friendly home in New Mexico.

people live all the time. These people do not have access to service from an electrical grid or cannot afford to pay for it.

Still more people have only limited electrical service. Their electricity may work only some of the time. To get power when they don't have electricity, they use generators. These machines can power everything from lamps to televisions. But they are noisy, and they pollute the air. They can also be expensive to run.

Most people without a steady supply of electricity live in poor countries. Many are in remote areas. Poor countries don't have the money to run power lines to people in remote areas. How can these people get cheap, reliable electric service? Some are getting it with the help of Earth-friendly energy sources such as solar power.

DEMAND AND SUPPLY

More people live in China than anywhere else. The country has about 1.3 billion people. China also has the world's fastest-growing economy. This means that people in China are beginning to earn more money. When population and wealth grow together, the demand for energy grows along with them.

China burns more coal for power than any other nation—about 2 billion tons (1.8 metric tons) a year. Still, this is not enough to supply the nation's growing energy demands. So the Chinese are turning to solar power for help.

Five thousand Chinese companies supply solar water heaters. These units run water through thin pipes that crisscross a smooth, shiny surface. The surface catches and holds the sun's heat. A typical unit costs about $330.

China burns more coal for power
than any other nation.

Even people who have electricity buy them, since solar power is cheaper than grid power. China leads the world in solar water heating units. About 30 million households use these systems.

PORTABLE POWER

What about electricity for people who don't stay in one place? Nomads who raise sheep, goats, and other livestock must move their animals to different grazing areas as the seasons change. How can these seasonal travelers bring electric power with them?

In China some nomads are buying portable rooftop solar panels. In Xinjiang, in northwestern China, forty thousand nomads and other rural people have bought them. A company called Shell Solar manufactures these panels. Bo Xiao Yuan of Shell says, "Nomads, they keep moving all year round. Grid power cannot be available everywhere, so [renewable energy provides] a very suitable way of life."

22

People who had been using smoky, dirty oil lamps at night now get their light from bright, clean electric bulbs. Each portable solar unit can also power a radio, a TV, and even a small heater.

The portable units have other uses as well. Gulinar Sitkan, a sheepherder from Xinjiang, has mounted solar-powered lights to the top of her yurt—a portable,

HOW LONG WILL IT LAST?

The sun is about 4.5 billion years old. Scientists estimate that the sun still has enough energy left to go on shining for the next 5 billion years before it finally burns itself out.

This Mongolian woman uses two portable solar panels, mounted to the side of her yurt, to provide energy for her family's needs.

circular tent made of wood and animal skins. Wolves used to snatch her sheep at night while she slept. Now the solar lights keep them away.

COOKING WITH SUNLIGHT

For two billion people in poor countries, the simple act of cooking a meal or boiling water to purify it is a struggle. Without electricity or natural gas, they can't turn a switch or press a button to heat an oven. Instead, they must spend up to seven hours each day searching for wood to fuel a fire.

Young girls usually help with the cooking, including looking for firewood. But that doesn't leave them much time to go to school or play the way girls in wealthier nations do. Could solar heat free them from all this work?

Food starts cooking at about 180°F (82°C). Water can be purified by heating it at 150°F (66°C) for ten minutes. How can heat from the sun produce temperatures this hot?

The answer is a portable oven that runs on solar energy. A solar oven is a simple device. An insulated box is lined with aluminum foil and covered with a pane of glass. Sunlight enters through the glass. The foil absorbs and reflects the light. The glass keeps the trapped heat from reflecting back out, just like the glass in a greenhouse.

As long as the sun keeps shining, the trapped heat remains in the box to cook the food, slowly but surely. Temperatures inside a solar oven range from 200 to 270° F (93 to 132° C). A meal takes two to four hours to cook in a solar oven. Boiling water for tea takes about half an hour.

CATCHING ON

The solar oven is not a new invention. British explorer John Herschel used a solar oven to cook food during an expedition to Africa in the 1830s. Now low-cost models have been developed for people in poor countries.

Many different types of solar devices can be used for cooking. This Bhutanese woman uses a solar cooking device to warm a meal on a sunny day.

Volunteers from environmental groups travel to these nations and introduce the ovens to people in remote villages.

The idea of solar cooking is catching on, especially in African nations such as Kenya. For example, volunteers from the environmental group Earthwatch brought solar ovens to the Kenyan market town of Zombe. They showed people how to put the ovens together and how to use them. After cooking and eating a few meals with the volunteers, the town's people were convinced. Here was a far simpler, cleaner, healthier way to cook food. Now the community of Zombe is building solar ovens of its own and selling them to other Kenyan towns.

A SILVER BULLET?

Solar power is free energy. It's also very abundant. The sun produces far more energy than we could ever use. Solar power is clean as well. Using solar power instead of fossil fuels means that no greenhouse gases or other pollutants get into the air. That's the positive side of solar power.

But here's the negative side. Solar power can be expensive. It costs lots of money to manufacture and hook together enough solar panels to make a solar power plant. Once a solar plant is up and running, it is cheaper to operate than a plant that burns fossil fuels. But the cost to open a solar plant is very high.

Then there is the problem of reliability. There is no place on Earth where the sun always shines. Solar energy is unpredictable. Developing more efficient collectors to capture more energy when the sun is shining will help. So will building better batteries to store more of that energy.

But this will not happen overnight. We can't look forward to a time in the near future when solar power will supply all our energy needs. For now, solar energy is not the silver bullet, the one simple, guaranteed solution to our energy problems. It is only part of the solution. Another part is wind power.

CHAPTER THREE

WIND POWER

Wind energy is nothing new. People have used wind power to drive ships since ancient times—before they knew what wind was or where it came from. Today we know that wind is a form of solar energy. Winds blow because the sun's heat strikes Earth unevenly.

> Wind energy is nothing new. People have used wind power since ancient times.

UNEVEN RAYS

The sun's rays hit Earth more directly and with greater intensity in the tropics—the area near the equator. As a result, the air in the tropics is very warm. Warm air rises. The rising air creates a zone of low pressure below it. Wind results from differences in air pressure. Air keeps flowing from areas of high pressure to areas of low pressure.

Eventually the warm air reaches the "ceiling" of the troposphere—the lowest part of Earth's atmosphere. From there it can rise no farther. Then it spreads out and flows north and south toward the poles. As these air currents travel along, they encounter hills, valleys, mountains, and trees. When air currents strike these irregular land features, the air responds by rising, falling, and changing direction. This creates more wind.

A sailboat catches the wind in its sails. Simple technology to capture wind energy has been used for thousands of years.

Temperature is also a factor. During the day, the land heats up faster than do oceans, rivers, and lakes. The hot air rises, creating an area of low pressure. Cool air moves in. The result is a cooling sea breeze, with wind blowing in from the water. During the night, the land cools off faster than the sea. Then cool air comes down, creating an area of higher pressure. The result is a land breeze, blowing out toward the water.

> ## RIDDLE
>
> **How is air in the atmosphere like water in the ocean? Warm air and warm water both tend to rise. Cool air and cool water tend to fall.**

Finally, the rotation of Earth plays a part. As winds blow north and south toward the poles, they are affected by Earth's rotation. In the Northern Hemisphere, air currents are turned to the right. In the Southern Hemisphere, Earth's rotation turns them slightly to the left. All these factors combine to keep Earth's air moving constantly.

Altogether, these factors power a global atmospheric system that flows like an ocean of air. In this constantly moving ocean, hot air rises and cold air sinks. The result is a never-ending flow of hot and cold air that we call wind energy.

WIND TURBINES

Wind turbines are the key to converting wind energy to electrical power. Wind turbines have big rotating blades. The blades are on top of a tower. As the blades turn, they spin the turbine's shaft inside the tower. The shaft is connected to a generator that makes electricity.

Wind power plants—also known as wind farms—have many wind turbines. The turbines at wind farms are very tall. Tall wind turbines produce a great deal of energy. That's because wind speed increases with altitude—and the higher the wind speed, the more energy there is to be captured.

Some wind farms have dozens of towers. Others have hundreds. Most wind farms are built on land. Some are built at sea.

ONSHORE WIND FARMS

Ridges and hills are windy places. This makes them good locations for wind farms. As air is forced over a ridge or hill, it picks up speed. That means more wind energy hits the blades of wind turbines.

Seashores are good places for wind farms as well. They tend to be windy because the uneven rate at which land and sea heats or cools sets air currents in motion.

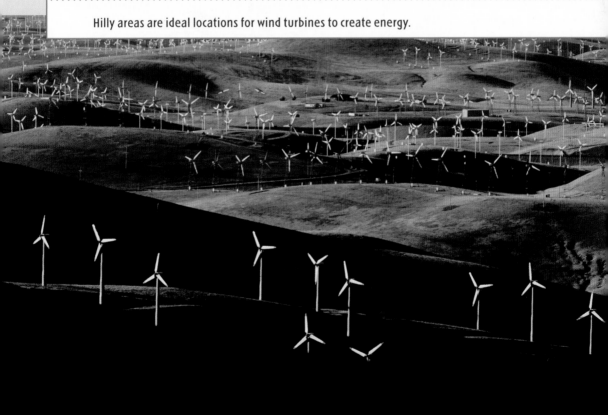

Hilly areas are ideal locations for wind turbines to create energy.

As of 2007, forty different U.S. states either had onshore wind farms or were planning to build them. The largest onshore wind farm in the world is Horse Hollow Wind Energy Center in central Texas.

OFFSHORE WIND FARMS

Offshore wind farms are more difficult to build and maintain due to the sea's enormous power. Some are operating in Europe. At present no offshore wind farms are in the United States. But that could change.

Cape Wind may become the United States' first offshore wind farm. If constructed, it will be located in Massachusetts, off the shore of Nantucket. According to plan, 130 wind towers will operate. The towers will bring electrical power to thousands of homes.

THE BIGGEST TURBINES

The world's largest wind turbines are in an offshore wind farm in the Scottish North Sea *(below)*. The rotor blades are 413 feet (126 m) long—the length of two entire soccer fields!

WINDMILLS

Windmills are a very old technology. People have been using these wind-powered machines for centuries. Windmills were used as far back as 200 B.C., when people in China and the Middle East relied on them to pump water and grind grain.

The Cape Wind site was chosen because the wind is strong, the water level is shallow, and waves are usually low. The location seemed perfect. But there are problems. As with any big energy project, Cape Wind must be approved by local, state, and U.S. governments. In October 2007, Massachusetts' Cape Cod Commission slowed things up. Cape Wind wanted to connect the wind farm to the state's power grid through electric cables. The commission said no. That leaves Cape Wind's future uncertain for now.

SMALL-SCALE WIND POWER

Like solar panels and collectors, some wind power units are made for individual use. These small wind turbines provide electricity for homes

A small wind turbine sits atop a home near Chorley in Lancashire, England.

in remote areas. The turbines are lightweight and compact. They can easily be mounted on rooftops. They can be used with diesel generators and solar units to supply all of a family's electricity.

Daniel Scott of northern Los Angeles County in California installed three units on his rural property. He expects that within seven years, he will have saved enough money on his electric bills to make up for the cost of building his little wind farm. After that he'll be getting his electricity for free.

NIMBY

Like solar power, wind power has its own set of problems. One problem is the appearance and location of the towers. They are huge. And they usually are on hilltops and seashores—places known for their natural beauty. "Shadow flicker" is also a problem. As the huge blades turn, they cast constantly moving shadows across the land.

When residents hear about plans to build a wind farm nearby, many object. This reaction is known as NIMBY—not in my backyard. People often react the same way to plans for coal-fired power plants, landfills, and highways.

32

A SHINING STATUE

If you look at the Statue of Liberty at night, you will see wind power in action. Floodlights shine on the statue's torch, and air-conditioning keeps Miss Liberty's interior air cool and dry—thanks to electricity from wind energy.

Spinning turbines do not directly power the statue's lights or air-conditioning. But for every cent it costs to keep the lights burning and the air circulating, the U.S. government contributes a cent to wind farms in Pennsylvania and West Virginia. This exchange reduces the amount of electricity that must be produced by fossil fuels.

Wind turbines tower over the village of Klettwitz in Brandenburg, Germany.

They do not want to see the environment around them destroyed to build commercial structures.

People have another reason for objecting to wind towers. They reach high into the sky, up where birds fly. Seabirds and land birds are injured and killed when they fly into the swiftly turning blades. Supporters of wind power argue that fossil-fuel power plants kill far more birds and other wildlife by polluting the air and water. But no one denies that wind towers do some harm.

DEMAND AND SUPPLY

Wind power plants have one of the same problems that solar power plants do: they are not always reliable. Just as the sun does not always shine, the wind does not always blow. Often wind farms cannot generate enough electricity when consumers need it most.

DID YOU KNOW?

Texas, California, Minnesota, Iowa, and Wyoming are the U.S. states that generate the most wind power.

In Texas, for example, the hottest days are often the least windy. Yet those hot, still days are when people use a lot of electricity to run their air conditioners.

That's one reason why wind power, like solar power, is seldom used as a stand-alone electricity source. Instead, it's used to supplement the energy supplied by fossil-fuel power plants. Like solar power, wind power by itself is no silver bullet. But it is a promising part of the solution to replacing fossil fuels.

34

DOING THE MATH

Wind power is the fastest-growing type of Earth-friendly energy on the planet. Between 1999 and 2005, it grew by 400 percent. How much electricity is generated by wind power worldwide?

In 2005 the total was 58,982 megawatts. On the average, 1 megawatt of wind power can serve about 160 U.S. households. Let's do the math: 160 x 58,982 = 9,437,120 households worldwide powered by wind energy.

Which nations have taken the lead? Denmark is way out in front. Wind power provides about 30 percent of that country's total demand for electricity. The other leading nations are Spain (9 percent) and Germany (6 percent).

DEVELOPING NATIONS

Denmark, Spain, and Germany are wealthy, developed countries. But wind power is growing in developing nations such as China and India too. With their fast-growing economies, they are on the lookout for alternatives to power from fossil fuels. Why?

Costs of coal, oil, and natural gas are climbing. And the electrical grids in these nations are often old and out of date. Old electrical grids are not as reliable as newer systems. They also cause more air pollution.

Developing nations are turning to wind energy in a big way. In 2005 wind power use rose 65 percent in China and 48 percent in India. Even remote areas of these nations are benefiting. The town of Khori, India, is one example.

Khori is in a hilly area where cars are a rare sight. The farmers of Khori still plow the land the way their fathers and grandfathers did, with handheld plows pulled by oxen. Yet electrical power there is ultramodern, drawn from a brand-new wind farm. There are three hundred towers in all, each one taller than a twenty-story building, with blades 100 feet (30 m) long.

35

A worker in Khori, India, carries a part for a wind turbine that provides electricity for the area.

CHAPTER FOUR

WATER POWER

Water power is the king of renewable energy. Hydroelectric power plants produce 97 percent of all the electricity produced by Earth-friendly energies. Worldwide, hydroelectric power supplies about 20 percent of all electricity. In the United States, it's 10 percent.

But how in the world do you get electricity from water? (One thing we all know: electricity and water don't mix.) It sounds dangerous—but it's not.

Water power is the king of renewable energy.

ELECTRICITY FROM WATER

One way to create electricity from flowing water is to build a dam. The dam controls the flow of water in the river, letting some of the water through. The rest of the water builds up behind the dam to form a lake. That's the reservoir.

The higher the water level rises in the reservoir, the higher the water sits above the river below. All that held-back, raised-up water is stored-up energy, ready for use.

Down near the bottom of the dam on the reservoir side is an intake pipe, aimed downward. When the pipe is opened, water from the reservoir flows down through it into the penstock—a pressurized pipeline inside the dam.

Tennessee's Cherokee Dam (*shown below*) was built to supply hydroelectric power during World War II (1939-1945). The dam still operates in modern times.

CAUTION: DAM OPENING!

It is not a good idea to stand in the water right below a dam when water is released. When opened, dam gates can quickly turn a calm river into a raging torrent.

At the end of the penstock is a turbine that looks like a wheel. It has bucket-shaped blades around its rim. The high-pressure water hits the blades and turns the turbine, generating electricity for the grid to transport to consumers.

Meanwhile, the water keeps going past the turbine and back out into the river below the dam. The water and the electricity never meet, so there's no danger. That's how you get electricity from water.

ONE DAM, THREE STATES

Water power can change the course of history. Hoover Dam has been called one of the great engineering works of all time. This massive concrete structure is on the Colorado River. It's on the border between Arizona and Nevada. The dam took five years to build. At 726 feet (221 m) tall, it is the second-highest

Hoover Dam (*shown above*) supplies hydroelectric power for the United States' southwestern region. The dam's reservoir, Lake Mead, backs up 110 miles (180 km) behind the dam.

dam in the United States. The dam's hydroelectric works produce power for Arizona, Nevada, and California.

Hoover Dam opened in 1936. Before then very few people lived in the southwestern United States. The lack of affordable electricity kept most prospective residents away. But with the rise of hydroelectric power, residents and businesses began moving to the area.

Besides providing electricity to the Southwest, Hoover Dam also helps control flooding. When heavy rains fall, the dam's reservoir, Lake Mead, can take in the extra water. That keeps the Colorado River from overflowing its banks and flooding the land.

THE VERY FIRST HARD HAT

The first hard hats were invented by Hoover Dam's construction workers. They were made of two baseball caps dipped in tar and set aside to harden.

39

Hoover Dam has been called one of the great engineering works of all time.

OCEAN TIDAL POWER

The pull of the sun and moon causes tides. Earth's rotation plays a part as well. Each day coastal areas along oceans get four tides—two high tides and two low tides. Along the shore, tidal water levels can rise and fall as much as 40 feet (12 m). That makes ocean tides a powerful source of Earth-friendly energy.

How can we harness all that energy to make electricity? One way is by building a tidal barrage. A tidal barrage is a kind of power plant. It consists of a dam built across an inlet—a narrow bay or cove. Gates are installed on the dam with doors that can be opened to allow water to enter or leave. Then a turbine system is installed behind the dam.

During high tides, the rising water enters the gates. During low tides, the water exits. As it enters and exits, the water turns the turbines, producing electricity.

OCEAN WAVE POWER

Wind blowing across the sea makes waves. This water movement can generate energy. The coasts of small islands and large landmasses make good sites for harnessing wave energy.

On the shoreline of the small Scottish island of Islay, for example, sits a wave power station called Limpet. The station's air-filled chamber has an opening at the bottom through which waves can enter. As the water pushes into the chamber, it compresses the air inside. As the water flows back out, the pressure drops.

40

The Limpet station was designed to blend into the shoreline.

The moving waves produce bursts of high-pressure air. These bursts drive a turbine connected to a generator that produces electricity.

KING WATER

Water power generates more electricity by far than any other Earth-friendly source. How did water power become king? For one thing, water is always available. Solar and wind power can be unpredictable. But water power is constant. Rivers keep running, tides flow in and out, and waves rise and fall twenty-four hours a day, seven days a week.

Another reason is the density of water. Water is far denser than air. Its molecules are massed much more tightly together. And more mass means more impact. A square foot (0.1 sq. m) of moving water hits turbine blades with far more force than a square foot of moving air does. More force means the turbine moves faster and creates more electricity.

DAM DAMAGE

Water power may be king, but it isn't perfect. Hydroelectric power plants can cause environmental damage. Since dams block rivers, they make life hard for fish. The rotating blades of turbines in rivers kill fish that get caught in them. Dams across rivers also upset the natural life cycle that fish must go through to survive. Salmon in the Pacific Northwest, for example, must journey upstream to specific spots to spawn, or reproduce and lay eggs. If a dam gets in their way, they can't make that journey. Then salmon

A fish ladder on the Columbia River helps salmon past the John Day Dam in Rufus, Oregon.

populations plummet. This also makes life difficult for the American Indian tribes who base their livelihoods on salmon fishing.

It is illegal in the United States to build dams that block fish migration and kill fish with turbines. Dam builders must set up systems that divert fish around the dam so that they can continue on their way without harm.

THREE GORGES

Imagine that you live near a river. Imagine that a dam for a hydroelectric plant is scheduled to be built there. Should you be worried? About 1.3 million Chinese people had a right to be worried when the Three Gorges Dam was planned and built.

China's Three Gorges Dam is five times the size of Hoover Dam. It was completed in 2006. This mammoth project spans the world's third-longest river, the Chang. The dam is 1.2 miles (2 km) wide and towers 607 feet (185 m) above the river.

The problem with the dam is its reservoir. The reservoir stretches more than 370 miles (600 km) up the river. This stretch of river used to be home to 1.3 million people. But the land was flooded when the reservoir was built. So now the people are gone and their houses are underwater. They had to abandon their land, move to higher ground, and start their lives over.

And the problems with the reservoir don't stop there. Along the same stretch of river were hundreds of factories, mines, and waste dumps. They are now underwater and severely polluting the river.

The extent of this pollution can be seen five months out of the year, during the time when the dam has been opened to lower the reservoir level. The level is lowered to prepare for extra water that will come from summer floods. With most of the water gone, the reservoir consists of miles of muck infested with industrial pollution. This area quickly turns into a breeding ground for flies, mosquitoes, and bacteria, endangering the health of people living nearby.

MICRO-HYDRO POWER

Micro-hydro projects do far less damage to wildlife, people, and the environment. These projects involve small dams and turbines that provide much smaller amounts of power. They provide electricity to small, isolated communities.

A micro-hydro plant in King Cove, Alaska, for example, gets power to all the town's seven hundred residents. King Cove is a remote fishing village, far from the electrical grid. The plant is powered by the area's abundant rainfall and meltwater from glaciers.

Some micro-hydro projects don't involve dams and reservoirs. These plants are called run-of-the-river plants. Water flows through the plant at just about normal speed. Part of the river's water is diverted and used to drive the turbine. These plants do very little damage to the environment.

THE WORLD'S LARGEST

The world's largest hydroelectric project is South America's Itaipu power plant. About one-fourth of the electrical power for Brazil and three-fourths of Paraguay's power come from the Itaipu plant.

CHAPTER FIVE

EARTH POWER

How are a volcano, a hot spring, and a geyser alike? They all show geothermal energy in action. Geothermal energy draws on the heat produced deep within Earth. When allowed to flow continuously to Earth's surface, this heat can create energy.

Earth is a sphere made of layers. The inner core is mostly made of solid iron. Then comes an outer core of liquid iron. The next layer, the mantle, contains molten rock. Geothermal energy can be seen in places where this liquid rock has flowed all the way through the outer layer, the crust. This happens when a volcano becomes active. When volcanoes erupt, they spew thick, red-hot streams of liquid rock called magma.

44

SUPERHEATED WATER

Magma makes its way to Earth's surface through cracks in solid rock. In places where magma has moved close to Earth's surface, the solid rock around it can get very hot. When water seeps down into cracks in this hot rock, it heats up.

Water superheated by hot rock can reach temperatures of 300°F (148°C). How hot is that? It's much hotter than boiling water. Water boils at 212°F (100°C).

EARTH'S HOTTEST HOT SPOT

Scientists estimate that the temperature at Earth's core is a supersizzling 7,200°F (4,000°C).

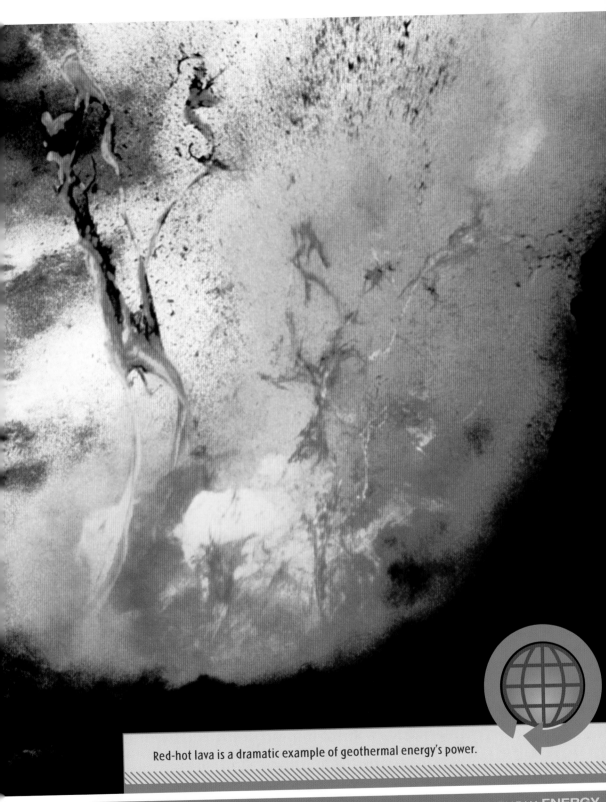

Red-hot lava is a dramatic example of geothermal energy's power.

The Grand Geyser in Yellowstone National Park can shoot giant plumes of water as high as 200 feet (60 m) into the air.

Sometimes superheated water comes bubbling up through a crack in Earth. The result is a hot spring. Or it might explode out of Earth, shooting high into the air in a geyser.

46

HEAT MINING

Volcanoes, hot springs, and geysers all happen naturally, without human action. But humans can also probe into Earth and pull geothermal energy from it. This is called heat mining.

The first step is to drill holes down to where the rock is hot. Hot rock is usually too far down for drills to reach. But a few places on Earth have hot rocks that are close to the surface.

Many of those places are near a fault line—a place where Earth's rocky surface is fractured. Scientists use high-tech remote sensing technology to locate those hot places. When they find a likely spot, drilling crews start to work. If all goes well, they end up with a pair of wells connected at the bottom by a hollow space that becomes a reservoir.

Then cool, dense water is poured down one well. As it falls, it runs through the hot rocks. By the time it hits bottom and flows into the reservoir, the water is superheated. The superheated water is pumped up the second well to the surface.

Up on top, a power plant takes in the water, turns it into pressurized steam, and shoots it at a steam turbine. The steam turns the turbine that powers generators that make electricity. After the steam cools back into water, it is pumped back down the first well. Then the process is repeated.

Other geothermal power plants tap directly into cracks in Earth that are filled with a constant supply of steam. These are called dry steam plants. They use the steam directly to drive steam turbines.

A PROBE TO THE CORE

Astronomy professor Dave Stevenson of the California Institute of Technology believes a probe could be sent all the way to the center of Earth. It would be surrounded by molten iron that would melt its way straight down. As the probe traveled, it would send back information on the temperatures and rocks around it.

GEOTHERMAL ADVANTAGES

What are the advantages of geothermal energy? A geothermal power plant works like a coal-fired plant, but no fuel is burned to heat water into steam. This means that geothermal plants release no polluting gases.

Geothermal energy is reliable too. A geothermal power plant can work day and night without stopping, much like a hydroelectric plant.

Finally, plenty of geothermal energy is down there to meet all the world's energy needs. We just don't have the technology to get at it yet.

GEOTHERMAL POWER IN THE WORLD

More than two hundred geothermal energy facilities operate in more than twenty countries around the world. These facilities provide power for more than 60 million people. In the United States, about seventy plants are operating. Most are in the southern and western states.

The most famous U.S. geothermal spot is called the Geysers. It is the world's largest complex of geothermal power plants. It has twenty-one power plants in all. The Geysers generates power for one million homes in northern California, from San Francisco north to the Oregon border.

Another type of geothermal operation is at work in the Southern California city of San Bernardino. Earth-heated water from below the ground is brought

48

The Calpine Sonoma power plant in the Geysers area of California produces electricity from geothermal energy.

Bathers relax in temperate waters outside a geothermal power plant in Iceland.

directly up and pumped out through pipes to heat dozens of the city's downtown buildings.

Which country relies the most on geothermal power? Iceland—just south of the arctic circle near Greenland. This island nation gets 90 percent of its heat and 25 percent of its electricity from geothermal sources.

CHAPTER SIX

BIOFUELS

Biofuels are another alternative energy option. Biofuels are all about powering transportation. While the other Earth-friendly energy sources are mainly alternatives to coal, oil, and natural gas, biofuels are substitutes for gasoline.

Biofuels can be made out of just about any kind of crop, from corn to grass to sugarcane. Crops are the key to biofuels' Earth friendliness. Like all plants, crops use CO_2 to make food. They absorb it from the atmosphere. In this way, crops may help to combat global warming.

Biofuels are all about powering transportation.

ETHANOL

Ethanol is the most widely used fuel made from crops. Ethanol is alcohol made from corn kernels. Unlike gasoline, ethanol can't power a car all by itself. But it can be added to gasoline to help a car or truck run.

In many places, ethanol is added to all gasoline at a rate of about 10 percent. A number of different kinds of cars and trucks also run on E85. This fuel contains 85 percent ethanol.

THIS BUS SMELLS LIKE LUNCH

Diesel-fueled cars and buses can be converted to run on recycled vegetable oil used to fry french fries. The exhaust smells just like those french fries.

Background image: A field of corn thrives under bright blue skies. *Bottom right:* A motorist uses recycled cooking oil to fill the tank of her car. The car has been specially designed to run on either vegetable oil or diesel fuel.

Corn must be harvested using polluting farm machinery.

Ethanol is a growing industry. More and more U.S. gas stations sell fuel that is largely ethanol. Not everyone likes it, though. Why?

The corn that is used to make ethanol is grown in fields planted and harvested by farm machinery. This machinery runs on fossil fuels. This leads critics of ethanol to say that the biofuel may actually be adding to global warming. Also, the fertilizers and insecticides needed to grow corn contain ingredients made from oil. When rain washes them off the land, they pollute rivers and streams. Furthermore, farmers must clear land to grow corn. Clearing land releases greenhouse gases. And it destroys natural landscapes and harms many plants. These plants absorb plenty of CO_2—in fact, they often take in more of the gas than corn does.

Fuel made from switchgrass provides an alternative to corn-based ethanol.

ALTERNATIVES TO CORN

Before the settlers arrived, switchgrass covered much of North America. Also known as panic grass, switchgrass can grow 9 feet (3 m) tall. Its roots go just as deep.

Switchgrass has been called a living solar battery. That's because it's very effective at storing energy from the sun. Switchgrass and other prairie grasses could be used in place of corn to make a biofuel called cellulose ethanol. Cellulose ethanol could be more Earth friendly than conventional ethanol because the grasses used to make it aren't as hard on the land as corn is.

Biofuels and the other alternative energies will replace fossil fuels one day, before those nonrenewable fuels run out—at least, that's the plan. Meanwhile, the work to reach that goal continues.

SWALLOWED UP

Imagine getting swallowed up in a sea of grasses. That's what pioneers said could happen to a man when he rode through the tall, thick prairie grasses that used to cover the Great Plains.

CHAPTER SEVEN

INTO THE FUTURE

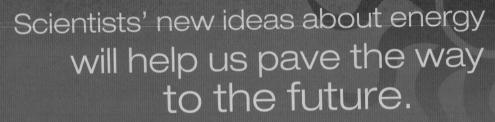

Every scientist dreams of discovering a new technology that changes people's lives for the better. Some dreams are small in scale and practical. They focus on down-to-earth ideas. Other dreams are big and more far reaching. They may be unusual or even outlandish.

Big or small, unusual or plain, scientists' new ideas about energy will help us pave the way to the future. Let's take a look at some of the Earth-friendly energy ideas that scientists are working on now.

Scientists' new ideas about energy will help us pave the way to the future.

SOLAR SKINS

How about generating solar power for electricity as you stand, sit, or walk around outside? In the near future, we all may be turned into solar power collectors. How?

Scientists are working on creating solar-collecting clothing. In this design, shirts and jackets would function like solar panels, producing and storing electrical energy. The energy could be used to power cell phones, calculators, flashlights, and more.

Scientists are trying for the same result with buildings, cars, boats, and planes. The idea is to cover everything possible in thin solar "skins" that absorb and use the sun's rays. These efforts employ thin-film technology.

Left: Sun-collecting shingles cover the roof of the Brockweir & Hewelsfield Village Shop, an Earth-friendly store in Gloucestershire County, England. *Background image:* A man models a backpack equipped with solar cells that can be used for charging a laptop. *Bottom right:* A race car with a solar-collecting surface speeds along using energy from the sun.

For example, solar-collecting film might be added to shingles and siding, transforming a house into its own Earth-friendly energy provider. Or a car might be powered by its own solar-collecting painted surface. We may even find ourselves flying on solar-powered airplanes—free of fossil fuel pollution.

A KITE-POWERED BOAT

German engineers are testing a ship that uses a huge inflatable kite to help pull it across the ocean.

SOLAR POWER SATELLITES

The National Aeronautics and Space Administration (NASA) is working on one very big dream involving solar power. Their dream extends all the way to outer space. NASA scientists are developing a design for an orbiting solar power station.

NASA's orbiting station would consist of solar cells mounted on platforms. From the cells' positions up in space, they would collect energy from the sun. This energy would be beamed down to Earth as microwaves (high-frequency radio waves). Receiving antennae would collect the microwaves,

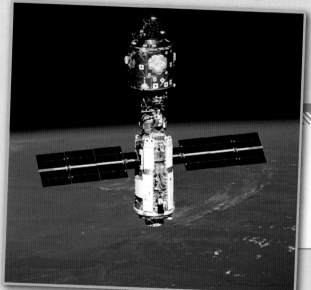

The International Space Station *(shown left)* allows NASA scientists to learn even more about space and new technologies that could improve people's lives. *Facing page:* An artist's rendition shows what a flying windmill would look like.

and special technologies would convert their energy to electricity for our homes. This idea may sound unbelievable. But then so did the idea of space travel not so many years ago.

FLYING WINDMILLS

Another Earth-friendly energy idea combines a very old technology—windmills—with a relatively new technology—flying. This idea was pioneered by Australian engineer Bryan Roberts. Roberts believes that flying windmills could be the answer to our energy problems.

Why does Roberts think that windmills should fly? Well, most of Earth's wind energy exists at altitudes of around 3 miles (5 km). Way up there, winds of more than 100 miles (160 km) per hour blow night and day. These are the smoothest, most powerful winds on the planet. If windmills could get at all this wind energy, they could generate more electricity than any earthbound turbine ever could.

Roberts's flying windmills would soar into the sky like helicopters. They'd be connected to long cables that anchored them to the ground.

The cables would supply electrical power to keep the windmills airborne. They would also transmit the electricity generated in the sky down to Earth for storage and eventual use by consumers. Roberts pictures a whole fleet of flying windmills soaring high in the air one day.

WAVE FARMS

Some scientists dream of harnessing the power of ocean waves to provide the world's electricity. Pelamis is a step in that direction. This project is under construction off the coast of Portugal. When finished and operating, Pelamis will become the world's first offshore wave power plant.

The name *Pelamis* comes from the scientific name for a surface-swimming yellow-bellied sea snake. And with its long system of metal tubing, Pelamis does look a bit like a snake. It has also been compared to a string of sausages or a line of rounded train cars hooked together.

58

The Pelamis device undergoes a test off the coast of Portugal.

Actually, Pelamis is made of strings of 400-foot (120 m) steel tubes. They float at sea 3 miles (5 km) off the coast. The tubes will move in response to the ocean's waves. Special equipment will channel that motion to generate electricity. No one can be sure whether Pelamis will work or whether it might become a hazard to passing ships. But the project looks promising. If it does succeed, Pelamis could be the first in a long line of wave farms drawing Earth-friendly energy from the endless ocean waves.

ELECTRIC TRASH

Another down-to-earth renewable energy dream looks as if it might succeed as well. This project is taking shape in a county on Florida's Atlantic coast. The county plans to build the first plant in the nation that gasifies trash. The heated gas will be used to create electricity.

Here's how it will work: Conveyor belts bring in garbage and dump it into containers. Below the containers is a chamber with machinery that creates a powerful charge of electricity. The charge is called a plasma arc. The plasma arc raises the temperature in the chamber to 10,000°F (5,538°C).

When the falling trash hits the plasma arc, the intense heat turns it into a gas. The trash molecules—which come from plants and animals—are broken down into atoms. Then the atoms come back together, but not in their original form. Instead of garbage, they are now harmless gases. The rest of the trash, mostly glass and metals, melts and then hardens into harmless, nontoxic materials.

The hot gases will be used to run turbines to produce electricity. The result: garbage is turned into electricity. It sounds like magic. County official Chris Craft called this project "the end of the rainbow" and said that "it will change the world."

A fuel-cell sport-utility vehicle parks at a hydrogen gas station in Berlin, Germany.

HYDROGEN FUEL CELLS

Yet another new Earth-friendly energy idea involves hydrogen fuel cells. A hydrogen fuel cell combines pure hydrogen with pure oxygen to produce electricity and water. No polluting gases are released into the air in this process.

The dream is to one day have cool, clean hydrogen fuel cells replace hot, dirty gasoline as the fuel that powers most of our vehicles. But there are problems.

First, electricity must be used to produce the hydrogen—and most electricity comes from fossil fuels. Second, hydrogen is highly flammable. The safety factor still needs work. Finally, there's the cost. Hydrogen fuel cells are too expensive for most consumers to afford. But if these problems can be solved, the hydrogen fuel cell dream just may come true.

NUCLEAR ENERGY

Finally, we can consider nuclear energy—a form of energy already used around the world to produce electricity. Nuclear energy does not add chemicals to the atmosphere or contribute to global warming. Some people see it as the energy source of the future.

But nuclear power is not really an Earth-friendly energy—at least, not according to most experts. Why not? Because nuclear power produces radioactive waste that is long lasting and deadly. No one has invented a foolproof way to dispose of this waste.

A terrible accident in 1986 showed the dangers of nuclear energy. The accident happened at the Chernobyl Nuclear Power Plant in the Soviet Union—fifteen republics that included Russia. On April 26, part of the Chernobyl plant exploded. The explosion released radioactive waste into the environment around the plant. Hundreds of thousands of people were killed or injured. People still suffer from deadly diseases caused by radiation released at the site.

The Chernobyl Nuclear Power Plant explosion was the worst nuclear accident in history.

This nuclear power plant under construction in France is expected to be up and running by 2012.

WHAT DO YOU THINK?

Is nuclear power clean and safe because it doesn't release any polluting gases into the air? Or is it dirty and deadly because of the radioactive waste it leaves behind?

WHAT NEXT?

Nothing like Chernobyl has happened since 1986—and nuclear energy remains quite popular outside the United States. There are 337 atomic reactors producing electricity in thirty countries. Around the world, 29 new plants are being built, and plans are in place to produce 64 more.

But in the United States, no new nuclear power plants have been scheduled for construction since Chernobyl. Still, the United States leads the world in nuclear power production. Nearly 20 percent of U.S. electricity comes from nuclear power.

Some experts are asking for more nuclear plants. Among them is biologist and author Stewart Brand, who believes that "the only technology ready to fill the gap and stop the carbon dioxide loading of the atmosphere is nuclear power."

Earth-friendly energies, along with nuclear power, offer real hope for cleaner energy sources in the future. We've seen how scientists, engineers, inventors, businesspeople, volunteers, and political leaders are trying to make Earth-friendly energy dreams come true. But what about you? How can you help?

63

GOING GREEN

The environment is everyone's responsibility. "Going green" means getting involved. How can you help protect the planet in general and promote Earth-friendly energies in particular? Here are some ideas to help you get started:

- **Plant trees.** Remember, trees and other green plants take in carbon dioxide that fossil fuels add to the air. Just one tree absorbs 2,000 pounds (900 kilograms) of CO_2 each year.

- **Unplug electrical devices when they're not in use.** Most computers, radios, TVs, and microwave ovens suck up electrical power even when you're not using them. By unplugging these energy vampires, you'll save more than 1,000 pounds (450 kg) of CO_2 each year.

- **Take shorter showers.** Showers account for two-thirds of all water heating costs. The less hot water you use, the less fossil fuel energy you consume. On average, you'll save about 350 pounds (160 kg) of CO_2 per year.

- **Use energy-efficient lights.** Replace the five lightbulbs you use most often at home, indoors and outdoors, with compact fluorescent bulbs. They use only one-third of the energy used by standard bulbs. If every household in the nation did this, we would save 1 trillion pounds (0.5 trillion kg) of greenhouse gases.

HOW TO WRITE TO YOUR LEGISLATOR

Writing to government leaders is a great way to communicate your concern about the energy issues affecting our environment. Anyone can send a letter to a senator or representative. Not sure where to start? Here are a few helpful hints:

- **Focus on a particular issue.** Are you concerned about pollution from cars and trucks? Do you support wind energy? Zeroing in on a specific issue will help give your letter focus.
- **Explain why the issue matters to you.** Write from your heart. Your letter doesn't have to be long or complicated. Just explain how you feel and use your own words.
- **Request a response from your legislator.** By requesting a response, you'll show that you are serious about the issue.
- **Be polite.** Make sure to use respectful language in your letter. And if your legislator follows up with a response, send a thank-you note. This will show that you value your legislator's time.

ENVIRONMENTAL GROUPS

Many organizations offer information about alternative energies. Here are just a few:

- **American Wind Energy Association**
  http://www.awea.org
  1101 14th St. NW, 12th Fl.
  Washington, DC 20005
  202-383-2500

- **Canadian Renewable Fuels Association**
http://www.greenfuels.org
31 Adelaide St. E.
PO Box 398
Toronto, ON
M5C 2J8
416-304-1324
- **Solar Energy International**
http://www.solarenergy.org
PO Box 715
76 S. 2nd St.
Carbondale, CO 81623
970-963-8855

GLOSSARY

biofuel: a gasoline substitute made from biological raw materials, such as corn or grasses

carbon dioxide (CO_2): a gas that is a mix of carbon and oxygen

climate: usual weather patterns, or the typical weather in a specific region

Earth-friendly energy: energy that is renewable and causes little pollution

fault line: a place where Earth's surface is fractured

fossil fuel: a fuel that formed underground from plants and animals that died millions of years ago

gasify: to turn into a gas

geothermal energy: natural heat energy from deep within Earth

global warming: the warming of Earth because of increased carbon dioxide and other heat-trapping gases in the atmosphere

greenhouse gas: a name for carbon dioxide and other polluting gases that hold the sun's heat near Earth. Greenhouse gases cause global warming.

photon: a particle of light and heat from the sun

renewable: something that cannot be used up

reservoir: a place where water is stored until it is needed

tidal barrage: a kind of power plant that uses energy from tides to produce electricity

troposphere: the lowest part of Earth's atmosphere

wind turbine: a machine with big rotating blades that sit on top of a tower. The rotation of a turbine's blades turns wind energy into electrical power.

67

SOURCE NOTES

18   "Transatlantic Weblog—Escaping a Chinese Tanker," *Transatlantic 21,* January 9, 2007, http://www.transatlantic21.org/home/blog-page/blog-detail/?tx_x4eblogdisplay_pi1%5Bpointer%5D=3&tx_x4eblogdisplay_pi1%5BshowUid%5D=33&cHash=36d2774b53&PHPSESSID=2721ef114b5a0186e8e7e9d832abf2a9 (February 4, 2008).

22   Bo Xiao Yuan, quoted in Lenora Chu, "China Nomads on Energy's Cutting Edge," *Christian Science Monitor,* August 31, 2006, http://www.csmonitor.com/2006/0831/p06s01-woap.html (February 5, 2008).

59   Chris Craft, quoted in Brian Skoloff, "County to Vaporize Trash, Sell Power to Grid," *MSNBC,* September 11, 2006, http://www.msnbc.msn.com/id/14718509/ (February 7, 2008).

63   Stewart Brand, "Environmental Heresies," *Technology Review,* May 2005, http://www.techreview.com/Energy/14406/page1/ (February 7, 2008).

SELECTED BIBLIOGRAPHY

BBC News. "Sea Machine Makes Waves in Europe." *BBC.* March 15, 2006. http://news.bbc.co.uk/2/hi/uk_news/scotland/4805076.stm#graphic (February 18, 2008).

Bender, Lawrence, Scott Z. Burns, Laurie David, and Lesley Chilcott. *An Inconvenient Truth.* DVD. Directed by Davis Guggenheim. Los Angeles: Paramount Classics, 2006.

California Energy Commission. *Energy Story.* April 22, 2002. http://www.energyquest.ca.gov/story/ (February 18, 2008).

Cleveland, Cutler J. "Three Gorges Dam, China." *Encyclopedia of Earth.* January 17, 2007. http://www.eoearth.org/article/Three_Gorges_Dam%2C_China (February 18, 2008).

EERE. "How Wind Turbines Work." *U.S. Department of Energy, Energy Efficiency and Renewable Energy.* November 30, 2006. http://www1.eere.energy.gov/windandhydro/wind_how.html (February 18, 2008).

Kocinski, Alexa Cosmo. "Cooking without Fire." *Solar Oven Society.* October 20, 2004. http://www.solarovens.org/news/ (February 18, 2008).

McNeill, J. R. *Something New under the Sun: An Environmental History of the Twentieth-Century World.* New York: W. W. Norton & Company, 2000.

Peterson, Erik, and Peter Madsen. "Wind Farm." *Encyclopedia of Earth.* July 31, 2007. http://www.eoearth.org/article/Wind_farm (February 18, 2008).

Worldwatch Institute. *State of the World 2006.* Edited by Linda Starke. New York: W. W. Norton & Company, 2006.

——. *Vital Signs: 2006-2007.* Edited by Linda Starke. New York: W. W. Norton & Company, 2006.

FURTHER READING

Alliance to Save Energy
http://www.ase.org/section/_audience/consumers/kids
Visit this site to learn what kids can do to make the world a more energy-efficient place.

Energy Kid's Page
http://www.eia.doe.gov/kids
This useful site includes interesting facts, games, and activities focused on energy.

Fridell, Ron. *Environmental Issues.* New York: Marshall Cavendish Benchmark, 2006. Read more about the issues that have an impact on our environment.

Johnson, Rebecca L. *Understanding Global Warming.* Minneapolis: Lerner Publications Company, 2009. Learn all about global warming and how it affects our planet.

Kids Saving Energy
http://www.eere.energy.gov/kids
On this site from the U.S. Department of Energy, you can learn about renewable energy, learn how you can save energy at home, and try several fun games and activities.

Saunders, Nigel. *Nuclear Energy.* Pleasantville, NY: Gareth Stevens, 2007. Saunders provides a clear and accessible discussion of nuclear energy.

Science Heroes
http://www.myhero.com/myhero/go/directory/directory.asp?dir=science
This page tells all about scientists who have pursued their dreams of making the world a better place.

Woods, Michael, and Mary B. Woods. *Environmental Disasters.* Minneapolis: Lerner Publications Company, 2008. Read more about environmental damage in this engaging selection.

INDEX

air currents, 26, 28–29. *See also* wind
    power: source of

batteries, 17–19, 25, 53
blackout. *See* power in poor
  countries

California, 15, 17, 32, 34, 39, 47–49
Cape Wind, 30–31
celebrities, 17
cellulose ethanol, 53
Chernobyl Nuclear Power Plant, 61–62
China, 6, 21–23, 31, 34–35, 42–43
coal-fired power plants, 6, 8–9, 32–34
coal sink, 6

Earth power. *See* geothermal power
Earthwatch, 25
electricity from garbage, 59
ethanol, 50, 52–53

flying windmills, 57–58

geothermal power: through dry
  steam plants, 47; through heat
  mining, 46–47; sources of, 44, 46;
  around the world, 48–49

geysers, 48

health problems, 9, 42–43, 61–62
Herschel, John, 24
Hoover Dam, 38–39, 42
Horse Hollow Wind Energy Center, 30
hydrogen fuel cells, 60

ice caps, 11
Iceland, 49

Kenya, 25
Khori, India, 35
King Cove, Alaska, 43

Limpet, 40–41

NASA (National Aeronautics and
  Space Administration), 56–57
NIMBY, 32–33
nomads, 22–23
nuclear energy, 61–63

offshore wind farms, 29–31

Pelamis, 58–59
portable power, 18–19, 22–25, 54, 56

power in poor countries, 20–25, 34–35

Roberts, Bryan, 57

Shell Solar, 22
solar power: for cooking, 23–25; in the future, 25, 54, 56–57; for heat, 20–24 ; for military, 18–19; panels, 15–19, 22, 25, 31; plants, 16–17, 25; satellites, 56–57, source of, 12, 14; for transport, 17–18
solar water heaters, 21–22
steam turbines, 8, 47
sun21, 17–18
switchgrass. *See* cellulose ethanol

thin-film technology, 54, 56

Three Gorges Dam, 42–43
tropics, 26

U.S. Army, 18–19

water power: availability of, 36; damage from, 41–43; from dams, 36, 38–43; in the future, 58–59; from ocean waves, 40–41; small-scale, 43; from tidal barrages, 39–40
wave farms, 39–41. *See also* water power: in the future
wind power: in the future, 34–35, 57–58; plants, 28–35, 57–58; problems with, 32–34, source of, 26, 28–29

71

ABOUT THE AUTHOR

Ron Fridell has written for radio, television, and newspapers. He has also written books about the Human Genome Project, including *Decoding Life: Unraveling the Mysteries of the Genome*. In addition to writing books, Fridell regularly visits libraries and schools to conduct workshops on nonfiction writing.

PHOTO ACKNOWLEDGMENTS

The images in this book are used with the permission of: © iStockphoto.com/Randy Plett, p. 1 (background and title); © iStockphoto.com/Alan Chao, pp. 1, 3 (top); AP Photo/Chiang Ying-ying, p. 3 (bottom); NASA/JSC, pp. 4-5; © Gala/SuperStock, p. 4 (inset left); © age fotostock/SuperStock, pp. 4 (inset right), 13, 29; © iStockphoto.com/Jarek Szymanski, p. 5; © Bill Barley/SuperStock, p. 7; © Charles Orrico/SuperStock, p. 8; © iStockphoto.com/Mark Evans, p. 9; © Bill Hauser/Independent Picture Service, p. 10; © Rolf Adlercreutz/Alamy, p. 11; NASA, pp. 12, 56; © Pacific Stock/SuperStock, p. 14; © Francisco Martinez/Alamy, p. 15; AP Photo/Solar Systems, HO, p. 16; © iStockphoto.com/Michal Rozanksi, p. 17; © Dylan Cross/AFP/Getty Images, p. 18; © Robert Nickelsberg/Getty Images, p. 19; © Alix Henry, p. 20; AP Photo/Greg Baker, p. 23; © Chris de Bode/Panos Pictures, p. 24; © George Glod/SuperStock, p. 27; AP Photo/Heribert Proepper, p. 30; © iStockphoto.com/Peter Austin, p. 31 (top); © Dave Ellison/Alamy, p. 31 (bottom); © PCL/Alamy, p. 32; AP Photo/Sven Kaestner, p. 33; AP Photo/Gautam Singh, p. 35; © Tom Brakefield/SuperStock, p. 37; Bureau of Reclamation, p. 38; Courtesy of Wavegen, p. 40; AP Photo/Yakima Herald-Republic, Gordon King, p. 42; © Photodisc/Getty Images, p. 45; © David Woodfall/WWI/Peter Arnold, Inc., p. 46; AP Photo/Calpine, p. 48; © Images&Stories/Alamy, p. 49; © iStockphoto.com/Purdue9394, p. 51; © Robyn Beck/AFP/Getty Images, p. 51 (inset); © Nigel Cattlin/Visuals Unlimited, p. 52; © Wally Eberhart/Visuals Unlimited, p. 53; © Mark Boulton/Alamy, p. 54; © Richard Levine/Alamy, p. 55; © Todd Strand/Independent Picture Service, p. 55 (inset); Courtesy Sky WindPower, p. 57; Courtesy of Pelamis Wave, p. 58; AP Photo/Michael Sohn, p. 60; AP Photo, p. 61; © Jean-Paul Barbier/AFP/Getty Images, p. 62.

Front Cover: © iStockphoto.com/Randy Plett (background, title and spine); © Photodisc/Getty Images (top left); AP Photo/Solar Systems, HO (right); © iStockphoto.com/Alan Chao (bottom left).

Back Cover: © iStockphoto.com/Randy Plett.